THE STORY OF THE
SACRAMENTO KINGS

THE NBA:
A HISTORY
OF HOOPS

THE STORY OF THE
SACRAMENTO KINGS

JIM WHITING

CREATIVE EDUCATION

Published by Creative Education
P.O. Box 227, Mankato, Minnesota 56002
Creative Education is an imprint of The Creative Company
www.thecreativecompany.us

Design and production by Blue Design
Art direction by Rita Marshall
Printed in the United States of America

Photographs by Corbis (Bettmann, Claro Cortes IV/
Reuters, Duomo, FRED THORNHILL/Reuters), Getty
Images (Andrew D. Bernstein/NBAE, Otto Greule/Allsport,
Walter Iooss Jr./NBAE, Neil Leifer/NBAE, Layne Murdoch/
NBAE, NBA Photo Library/NBAE, Dick Raphael/NBAE,
Rick Stewart, Justin Sullivan, Rocky Widner/NBAE),
Newscom (Song Qiong/ZUMA Press), USA TODAY Sports
(Malcolm Emmons)

Library of Congress Cataloging-in-Publication Data
Whiting, Jim.
The story of the Sacramento Kings / Jim Whiting.
p. cm. — (The NBA: a history of hoops)
Includes index.
Summary: An informative narration of the Sacramento
Kings professional basketball team's history from its 1945
founding as the Rochester Royals to today, spotlighting
memorable players and events.
ISBN 978-1-60818-447-7
1. Sacramento Kings (Basketball team)—History—Juvenile
literature. I. Title.

GV885.52.S24W55 2014
796.323'640979454—dc23   2013039663

CCSS: RI.5.1, 2, 3, 8; RH.6-8.4, 5, 7

First Edition
9 8 7 6 5 4 3 2 1

Cover: Center DeMarcus Cousins
Page 2: Guard Tyreke Evans
Pages 4-5: Guard Mitch Richmond
Page 6: Forward Maurice Stokes

TABLE OF CONTENTS

COURTSIDE STORIES

INTRODUCING...

OFF TO A
GREAT START

SACRAMENTO'S HISTORIC CALIFORNIA STATE CAPITOL WAS CONSTRUCTED IN THE 1800s.

n 1806, a Spanish expedition headed by Gabriel Moraga discovered a smooth-flowing river in central California. An expedition member wrote, "The air was like champagne, and [the Spaniards] drank deep of it, drank in the beauty around them. 'Es como el sagrado sacramento! [It's like the Holy Sacrament!].'" Moraga dubbed the river and surrounding valley Sacramento. Several decades later, the discovery of gold on the nearby American River ignited a feverish influx of people who hoped for instant wealth. John Sutter Jr.—son of one of the men who had made the initial discovery—established a trading colony on the Sacramento River to serve the miners, calling it Sacramento. Soon it became the first incorporated city in California and, within a few years, was named the state capital. Today, Sacramento is the sixth-largest city in California, and the metropolitan area has a population of more than 2.5 million.

AFTER YEARS OF RELOCATING, THE TEAM CELEBRATED TWO DECADES AT ITS SACRAMENTO HOME IN 2004.

Many of those gold rushers made transcontinental treks that included several stops along the way. So did the city's franchise in the National Basketball Association (NBA), the Sacramento Kings, which arrived in 1985. And like many of California's early settlers, the team boasts an especially colorful history.

In 1923, a high school hoops star in Rochester, New York, named Les Harrison formed two semi-pro teams sponsored by liquor companies, Seagrams and Ebers Brothers, soon after his graduation. The Rochester Seagrams were good enough to be invited to the 1940 and 1941 World Professional Basketball Championships in Chicago. Two years later, Harrison moved the team into a 6,400-seat arena. At the same time, he renamed it the Rochester Pros because local newspapers disliked giving free publicity to a liquor company by mentioning the team name in game stories.

Harrison sought out the best possible competition for his team, scheduling games against opponents such as the Harlem Globetrotters and New York Renaissance. In 1945, he had the opportunity to join the National Basketball League but Seagrams refused to support this effort. Harrison and his brother Jack borrowed enough money to buy

OTTO GRAHAM

STARS IN OTHER GALAXIES

The 1945–46 Royals NBL championship team received contributions from three players who went on to stardom in other fields: pro football quarterback Otto Graham, major-league baseball catcher Del Rice, and actor Chuck Connors. Graham was a college All-American in both football and basketball who played that one year with Rochester before turning his talents to football and leading the Cleveland Browns to seven championships in two leagues. Rice was a three-sport star in high school and signed a pro baseball contract soon after graduating. He played 4 seasons in Rochester, combining that with what became a 17-year major league career in which he received renown as a top-rated defensive catcher. Connors played college basketball, primarily as a backup. He filled the same role with both the Royals and later the Boston Celtics. "I wasn't a bad basketball player, but I was far from the world's greatest," Connors said. "Good defense, no offense, that was me." So it's somewhat ironic that Connors, who also played pro baseball, achieved his greatest fame as a sharpshooter in the television series *The Rifleman* (1958–63).

JACK TWYMAN

POSITION FORWARD
HEIGHT 6-FOOT-6
ROYALS SEASONS
1955–66

Along with fellow forward Maurice Stokes, Jack Twyman was one of the Rochester (and Cincinnati) Royals' best players in the late 1950s. Drafted in 1955 out of the University of Cincinnati, Twyman paired with Stokes to give the Royals a versatile and high-powered offense. He was a prolific scorer who averaged better than 20 points a game for 4 straight seasons from 1958–59 to 1961–62, using his ability to shake free of defenders with slick low-post moves to consistently earn high-percentage shots. Over the course of his 11-season career with the Royals, he averaged 19.2 points and 6.6 rebounds per game. The scrappy forward also gained distinction as the first player in NBA history to average more than 30 points a game for a season when he netted 31.2 points a night in 1959–60. "It was kind of a dream season for me," Twyman said. "It seemed like I had a big game every time we went out there." After his playing career came to an end, Twyman entered the broadcasting booth as an NBA television analyst.

a franchise. Les Harrison became a one-man band as coach, general manager, president, and marketing director. He launched a city-wide contest to name the team. The winner was 15-year-old Richard Paeth, who suggested the name Royals, asking, "What could be more fitting than this as a name for the team Les Harrison is going to send out to bring the crown to Rochester?"

The Royals became one of the best teams in the NBL, winning the league championship in their first season and losing in the finals the next two years. The team was led in those early seasons by such standouts as forward Arnie Risen and guard Bobby Wanzer. In 1948, the Royals were among four NBL teams to join the Basketball Association of America (BAA), reaching the Western Conference finals that year before being eliminated. In 1949, the franchise joined its third league when the BAA and NBL merged to form the NBA.

The NBA's first seasons were fruitful ones for the Royals, who featured guards Bob Davies and Red Holzman. The Royals were title contenders, but winning a championship meant getting past a powerful rival—the Minneapolis Lakers, who featured the league's most dominant big man, 6-foot-10 center George Mikan. Rochester could not overcome Mikan's size and strength in the low post, losing to Minneapolis in the 1949 playoffs. "When I started playing with Rochester, it was either us or Minneapolis that would win it all," Davies later said. "They had the big men, and we had the good little men. That was the difference in a nutshell. It was murder playing against Mikan,

because when the Lakers needed two points, he'd get them. George Mikan cost me a lot of money in playoff bonuses and endorsements."

In the 1951 NBA playoffs, Mikan was sidelined by a fractured leg. The Royals capitalized on the opportunity, beating the Lakers three games to one in the Western Division finals. Then, behind balanced scoring from Davies, Risen, and Wanzer, and Holzman's all-around contributions, the Royals defeated the New York Knicks four games to three to capture the league championship. Local media heaped praise on Harrison for his role in the success, with *Democrat and Chronicle* sportswriter Matt Jackson noting, "It's been quite an experience for a guy playing around with his own bankroll, stymied by a town which hasn't an adequate-sized arena in which to parade his high-priced and talented performers."

The Royals remained a force through the 1952–53 season but could not get past the division semifinals. Then, after disappointing losses in the division finals and semifinals the next two seasons, new talent arrived in Rochester in the form of rookie forwards Maurice Stokes and Jack Twyman. The pair, obtained in the 1955 NBA Draft, had great chemistry, but they did not bring immediate team success. The Royals posted losing records in 1955–56 and 1956–57, and attendance plummeted to about 2,000 fans per night. Facing such bleak circumstances, Harrison decided to seek greener pastures elsewhere. In 1957, the Royals moved to Cincinnati, Ohio.

Former Chicago Bulls guard Michael Jordan is generally considered to be the greatest player in NBA history. Before Jordan came along, Oscar Robertson was the most multitalented player in basketball. "The Big O" had quickness and explosive offensive moves, and he also dominated on the defensive end with his strength. Robertson essentially invented the concept of the "triple-double" (tallying double digits in 3 statistical categories in a single game) when he averaged 30.8 points, 12.5 rebounds, and 11.4 assists per game in 1961–62. It is considered a rare achievement for a player to record a triple-double in a game, yet Robertson averaged a triple-double every night in that incredible season and came very close to doing it again in the three seasons that followed. As of 2014, no NBA player had ever duplicated that feat. "He obviously was unbelievable, way ahead of his time," said Royals center/forward Jerry Lucas. "There was no more complete player than Oscar." In 1970, the Royals traded Robertson to the Milwaukee Bucks, where he teamed with star center Lew Alcindor to win the 1971 NBA championship.

THE "BIG O" ARRIVES

OSCAR ROBERTSON (#14) CONFIDENTLY TOOK ON SEVERAL CELTICS RIVALS AT ONCE.

The Royals were optimistic as they settled into Cincinnati, a community along the Ohio River nicknamed "The Queen City." Featuring the up-and-coming duo of Stokes and Twyman, the Royals also obtained powerful young forward Clyde Lovellette. The Royals finished a mere 33–39 and squeaked into the 1958 playoffs, where they lost to the Detroit Pistons in the first round.

The Royals stumbled to a 19–53 mark in 1958–59 and 19–56 the following season, generating whispers around the NBA that the team might fold. But Cincinnati's outlook improved dramatically when it obtained guard Oscar Robertson via the 1960 NBA Draft. Team officials hoped Robertson—a star at the University of Cincinnati—would attract more fans and help win a few more games, but they had no idea he would become one of the most dominant players in the game.

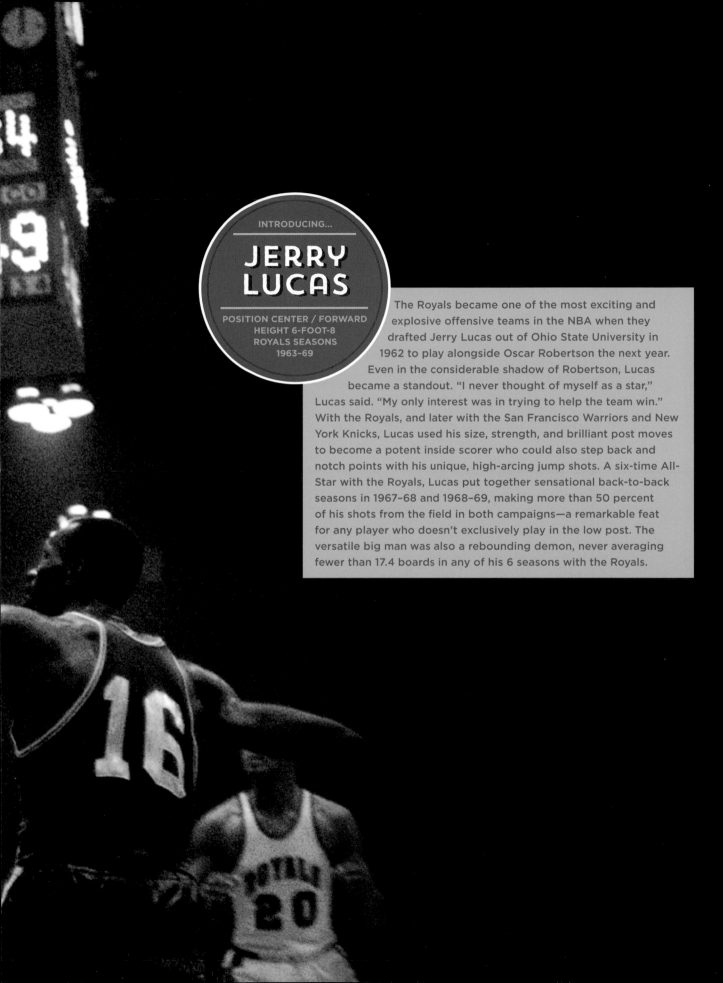

INTRODUCING...

JERRY LUCAS

POSITION CENTER / FORWARD
HEIGHT 6-FOOT-8
ROYALS SEASONS
1963–69

The Royals became one of the most exciting and explosive offensive teams in the NBA when they drafted Jerry Lucas out of Ohio State University in 1962 to play alongside Oscar Robertson the next year. Even in the considerable shadow of Robertson, Lucas became a standout. "I never thought of myself as a star," Lucas said. "My only interest was in trying to help the team win." With the Royals, and later with the San Francisco Warriors and New York Knicks, Lucas used his size, strength, and brilliant post moves to become a potent inside scorer who could also step back and notch points with his unique, high-arcing jump shots. A six-time All-Star with the Royals, Lucas put together sensational back-to-back seasons in 1967–68 and 1968–69, making more than 50 percent of his shots from the field in both campaigns—a remarkable feat for any player who doesn't exclusively play in the low post. The versatile big man was also a rebounding demon, never averaging fewer than 17.4 boards in any of his 6 seasons with the Royals.

Robertson was a player with no weaknesses. He was a solid ball handler, a fine passer, and a stout defender, and he could either swish shots from the outside or penetrate defenses for soaring dunks or layups. Perhaps most importantly, Robertson played with great confidence—a quality that inspired his teammates on a nightly basis. Nicknamed "The Big O," he finished his rookie season with stunning averages of 30.5 points, 10.1 rebounds, and 9.7 assists.

Robertson was even better the following season, averaging 11.4 assists to go along with 30.8 points and 12.5 rebounds as the Royals went 43–37. "Don't try to describe the man," said an awestruck Twyman. "You can watch him, you can enjoy him, you can appreciate him, but you can't adequately describe him. It's not any one thing—it's his completeness that amazes you." In the playoffs, however, Cincinnati fell to Detroit in the first round.

he Royals got even better in 1963 when they added Jerry Lucas. The former Ohio State University star could play center or forward, and he developed an immediate rapport with Robertson. The two led the Royals to a 55-25 record and another postseason berth. Cincinnati defeated the Philadelphia 76ers in a first-round matchup before losing the Eastern Division finals to the powerful Celtics in a five-game series.

Despite their playoff struggles, the Royals remained confident of their chances at an NBA title. "We knew we were a good team and had the talent to compete with the best teams in the league," Lucas explained. "We felt like we had the inside game and the outside game to give a great account of ourselves for 48 minutes. When we were at our best, we caused problems for everyone—Boston, Philadelphia, and the [Los Angeles] Lakers. We thought it was just a matter of time before we would get our turn."

Still, Cincinnati's postseason frustrations continued the next three seasons. Despite strong regular seasons from 1964 to 1967, the Royals suffered first-round playoff defeats. While the talent—headlined by Robertson, Lucas, guard Adrian Smith, and forward Happy Hairston—was undeniable, the Royals simply could not reach the ranks of the NBA's elite.

When Cincinnati fell to a losing record in 1969–70, former Celtics guard Bob Cousy became the new head coach. Although Cousy had been a Hall of Fame player, he would find little success as a coach. His hard-driving, demanding personality rubbed Robertson and Lucas the wrong way, and the Royals soon traded away both stars.

RED HOLZMAN

THAT CHAMPIONSHIP SEASON

The Kings franchise has won one NBA championship since joining the league in 1949. That title run came as the Rochester Royals in the 1950–51 season. The Royals beat the Fort Wayne Pistons and the Minneapolis Lakers to advance to the NBA Finals, where they faced the New York Knicks. The Royals won the first two games in Rochester before traveling to New York's 69th Regiment Armory and beating the Knicks on their home court to take a three-games-to-none lead. The Knicks, however, bounced back with three straight wins to force a pivotal Game 7 in Rochester. The Royals were shaky early on, and the game was tied at 75–75 when Rochester guard Bob Davies drained 2 free throws with 40 seconds remaining. The Royals clinched the title when forward Jack Coleman added a late layup for a 79–75 victory. "We thought we had the title, and then it almost slipped away," said guard Red Holzman (who would later lead the Knicks to two NBA championships as a coach). "But we came through at the end."

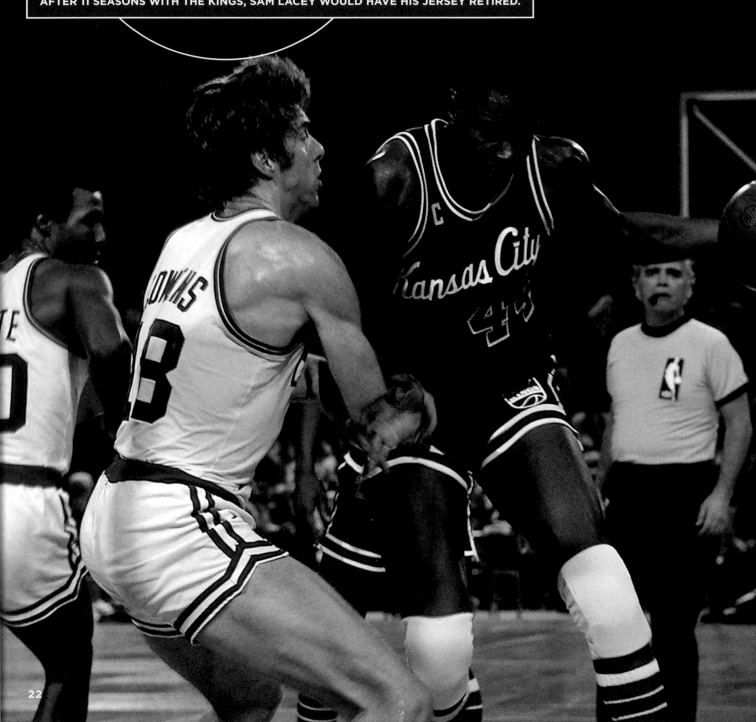

TINY COMES UP HUGE

AFTER 11 SEASONS WITH THE KINGS, SAM LACEY WOULD HAVE HIS JERSEY RETIRED.

The Royals began to develop a new core of stars in 1970 when they drafted super-quick point guard Nate Archibald. The Royals also brought in rookie Sam Lacey, a 6-foot-10 center with the size and strength to be a significant low-post presence. Although Lacey lacked the talent of the era's elite centers—such as Kareem Abdul-Jabbar, Wilt Chamberlain, and Willis Reed—he was strong enough defensively to make his All-Star rivals work hard for points and rebounds.

By 1972, the Royals weren't attracting enough fans to remain in Ohio. The team was sold to a group of businessmen from Kansas City, Missouri, and moved there before the start of the 1972–73 season. Since Kansas City's Major League Baseball team already had the name of Royals, the basketball franchise became the Kings to maintain the "royal" theme. In addition to games in Kansas

A LASTING FRIENDSHIP

When the Rochester Royals moved to Cincinnati in 1957, they looked like a team ready to challenge the dominant Boston Celtics for NBA supremacy. The main reason for optimism in Cincinnati was the stellar one-two punch of forwards Maurice Stokes and Jack Twyman, a couple of superb scorers who could also pass and defend. Stokes had won the 1956 NBA Rookie of the Year award and was widely recognized as one of the league's best players a year later. Sadly, his career was ended—and his life dramatically altered—when he fell to the floor during a game late in the 1957–58 season, hit his head, and suffered a brain injury that ultimately left him paralyzed and confined to a bed. Twyman, who had been friends with Stokes since the two were children, became Stokes's legal guardian and cared for his injured friend until Stokes died in 1970. "You'll never know, meet, or read about anybody as courageous as Maurice," said Twyman. "I never heard the man complain in 12 years of lying on his back."

City, the Kings also played about 15 games a season in Omaha, Nebraska, to widen their regional fan base and became the Kansas City-Omaha Kings.

Although the Kings went just 36–46 in their first season, Archibald emerged as one of the league's most exciting players. Officially listed at 6-foot-1 yet actually 5-foot-10, "Tiny" was a dynamic scorer who led the NBA in both points and assists that year. He put up huge numbers with long, rainbow jumpers and quick cuts to the hoop.

The Kings dropped the Omaha portion of their name in 1975 and began playing exclusively in Kansas City. In their continuing effort to build a talented young lineup, the Kings traded Archibald in 1976 for draft picks, which they used to obtain dynamic guards Otis

HEAD COACH COTTON FITZSIMMONS OFTEN KNELT COURTSIDE TO AVOID TECHNICAL FOULS.

THE UPSET KINGS

The Kansas City Kings were a mediocre team in 1980–81. Head coach Cotton Fitzsimmons was a likable leader who preached high-energy defense and the importance of sharing the ball, but his lessons seemed half-learned, as the Kings went just 40–42. That record, though, was good enough to get Kansas City into the playoffs, and Fitzsimmons's players suddenly began to heed their coach's instructions. Behind the outstanding guard duo of Otis Birdsong and Phil Ford, the Kings beat the Portland Trail Blazers in the opening round. That was a surprise, but the Kings pulled off a real shocker in the second round when they overcame the powerful Phoenix Suns, the Western Conference champion, thanks to the clutch shooting of forward Scott Wedman. However, Kansas City's dream of an NBA title died when the Royals lost to the Houston Rockets in the Western Conference finals, four games to one. "We thought we might make it all the way to the Finals, but Houston stopped us," said Ford. "But it was a great year all the way around."

PHIL FORD

"IN TERMS OF INDIVIDUAL TALENT, I THINK YOU WOULD HAVE TO SAY THERE IS NOT A LOT HERE. BUT OUR CLUB HAS CHEMISTRY. NOBODY'S GOING TO BEAT US BADLY IN THE PLAYOFFS."

— COTTON FITZSIMMONS ON THE 1978 KINGS

Birdsong and Phil Ford. In addition to working well together on the court, Birdsong and Ford became close friends off of it. Their shared sense of humor helped keep their teammates relaxed and upbeat. "They're like two peas in a pod," said Cotton Fitzsimmons, who took over as the Kings' coach in 1978. "They're a couple of professional comedians who just happen to play ball in the NBA. They're the guys who keep this team loose, and you have to be loose to play basketball."

he Kings won the Western Conference's Midwest Division in 1978–79 but lost to the Phoenix Suns in the first round of the playoffs for the first of two straight years. Two seasons later, the Kings went just 40–42 but hit their stride late in the year. As the postseason began, Fitzsimmons believed his team was ready to play its best ball. "In terms of individual talent, I think you would have to say there is not a lot here," the coach admitted. "But our club has chemistry. Nobody's going to beat us badly in the playoffs."

Fitzsimmons was right. The Kings beat the favored Portland Trail Blazers two games to one in the first round. Then they faced the Suns and jumped out to a three-games-to-one lead before Phoenix stormed back to tie the series at three apiece. With the decisive Game 7 in Phoenix, the Suns were favored. But the Kings played their best game of the series, stunning Phoenix 95–88 and advancing to the Western Conference finals. The Kings' Cinderella run ended there, though, as the highflying Houston Rockets won in five games.

INTRODUCING...
NATE ARCHIBALD

POSITION GUARD
HEIGHT 6-FOOT-1
ROYALS / KINGS SEASONS
1970–76

When the Cincinnati Royals traded Jerry Lucas in 1969 and Oscar Robertson in 1970, they needed a new star to grab the reins of the team and lead. That star came in the unlikely form of Nate "Tiny" Archibald. Although Archibald was short in stature (officially 6-foot-1 but actually three inches shorter), he had heart and talent in excess. After Archibald averaged 16 points per game as a rookie, Royals head coach Bob Cousy realized he had a special talent on his hands. In 1971–72, he made Archibald the focus of the team's offense. The guard responded by filling up the nets. Zipping around the court with incredible speed, Archibald averaged 28.2 points per game and won over fans not only in Cincinnati but throughout the league. The following year, Archibald was perhaps the NBA's best player, leading the league in both scoring (34 points per game) and assists (11.4 per game)—a feat no player had ever achieved before. "I was dedicated to the game," Archibald explained. "I only wanted to get better and help my team improve."

MOVING TO THE COAST

LARRY DREW DROVE AND DISHED AGAINST GREAT BLOCKERS SUCH AS LARRY BIRD (#33).

That memorable run would turn out to be the greatest—and last—highlight for the Kings in Kansas City. They returned to the playoffs in 1984 but were swept by the Lakers. During a 31–51 campaign the next season, the Kings faced a familiar problem—low fan attendance. In May 1985, the franchise headed west to Sacramento.

Although the Kings' new home was small by NBA standards, their new fans compensated by being extra loud. In the club's 1985–86 season home opener, Kings guard Larry Drew arrived early and was blown away by the enthusiasm of the crowd outside. "It reminded me of what you see before a college football game," he said. "It was like the boosters in the parking lot, barbecuing, throwing footballs around.... People were dressed in tuxedos, and some women were in evening gowns. They were really

CALIFORNIA CALLS

Stability is one thing every professional sports team needs, but it's a commodity that has escaped the Kings franchise throughout much of its history. In 1957, the franchise moved from Rochester to Cincinnati, and in 1972, it relocated to Kansas City. However, the franchise never was able to capture the full support of its home fans in any of the three locations. Fans fell in love with the team in all three cities when it played well, but attendance would evaporate during the difficult times. Prior to the 1985 season, Kings ownership moved the team to Sacramento. A city with a population less than one million at the time, Sacramento had no other pro sports franchise. The Kings opened their run in Sacramento before a full house on October 25, 1985, and the fans were ecstatic, even though the team dropped a 108–104 decision to the Los Angeles Clippers. Not only did fans fill the 10,333-seat ARCO Arena on a nightly basis, they did it with passion. "Those fans were crazy," recalled guard Reggie Theus. "They loved us, and they were loud every night."

HIGH-SCORING REGGIE THEUS RECORDED MORE THAN 6,000 ASSISTS DURING HIS CAREER.

getting geared up for their basketball."

The Kings were a high-scoring team in their first year in California's capital, averaging 108.8 points per game. Led by sharpshooting guards Eddie Johnson and Reggie Theus, Sacramento went 37–45 and made the playoffs, only to lose in round one. The Kings would struggle after that, failing to make the playoffs for the next nine seasons. Even the coaching leadership of former NBA greats Bill Russell and Willis Reed and the efforts of such players as center Joe Kleine, swingman Harold Pressley, and guard Danny Ainge could not propel the team over the hump.

In the early 1990s, the Kings suited up such quality players as forwards Antoine Carr and Wayman Tisdale, and long-range-bombing guard Mitch Richmond. Still, Sacramento remained a losing club. The team hit several low spots during the 1990–91 season. The Kings scored just 59 points in a 42-point loss to the Charlotte Hornets, the lowest output by an NBA team since 1955. They also closed the season with 37 straight road losses, a new NBA record.

Things finally started to turn around for the Kings in 1994–95, when they finished 39–43. Sacramento matched that mark the following season and even made the playoffs. The

INTRODUCING...

MITCH RICHMOND

POSITION GUARD
HEIGHT 6-FOOT-5
KINGS SEASONS
1991–98

Mitch Richmond was already a full-fledged NBA star by the time he arrived in Sacramento via trade in 1991. The guard had excelled with the fast-moving and high-scoring Golden State Warriors, but many fans thought Richmond's play would decline in Sacramento. Talent was scarce, and the team had long struggled. Richmond didn't regress; instead, he raised his level of play significantly as he was anointed the Kings' leader. Richmond was a lethal scorer with one of the most accurate jump shots the NBA had ever seen, and he led Sacramento in scoring in each of his 7 seasons there, making the All-Star Game every year but 1 and averaging at least 21.9 points, with a high of 25.9 in the 1996–97 season. For many years, he was the lone bright spot for a Kings team that lost often and was frequently blown out. "You're talking about a guy who persevered through some tough times in Sacramento," Kings team president Geoff Petrie said. "He was a great, great player and a great competitor—one for the ages."

franchise's outlook brightened further when brothers Joe and Gavin Maloof, a pair of wealthy hotel moguls, bought the team in 1997–98. The Kings put together a winning record the following year, going 27–23 in a season shortened by a labor dispute between owners and players.

In 1998, the Kings overhauled their roster, trading Richmond to the Washington Wizards for powerful forward Chris Webber, drafting exciting point guard Jason Williams, and picking up veteran center Vlade Divac as a free agent. Playing with greater chemistry and a new flair, the Kings enjoyed a winning season in 1999–2000 and really came into their own in 2000–

01, recording a 55–27 record that was fourth-best in the NBA. "We had something going, there's no doubt about that," Webber said. "We were in the process of becoming one of the most competitive teams in the league, and other teams had a hard time defending us. We had a lot of offensive options, and our confidence was growing. We liked playing together and thought it would be just a matter of time as to when we got our championship."

ROOKIE JASON WILLIAMS LOOKED TO CREATE CHEMISTRY AMONG HIS KINGS TEAMMATES.

CHRIS WEBBER LIVED UP
TO HIS ALL-STAR STATUS
DESPITE A FIRST-ROUND
PLAYOFF LOSS IN 2000.

PEAK
PERFORMANCE

EVEN STARS SUCH AS TRACY McGRADY WERE SHUT OUT BY THE KINGS' STRONG DEFENSE.

Sacramento's 2001–02 season was one to remember, as the Kings streaked to a stunning 61–21 record. With Webber scoring 24.5 points per game, swingman Peja Stojakovic netting another 21.2, and point guard Mike Bibby's slick ball-handling and passing, the Kings boasted one of the NBA's most versatile attacks. In the playoffs, the Kings cruised past the Utah Jazz and Dallas Mavericks in the first two rounds. Then they met the powerful Lakers in the Western Conference finals. Although Sacramento seized a three-games-to-two lead in the series with a 92–91 victory in Game 5, it could not seal the deal. The Lakers stormed back to win the next two games, concluding an especially physical and intense battle.

Unfortunately, the Kings had peaked. The core remained intact through the 2004–05 season, but the Kings fell in the first round of the playoffs. In 2005, Webber left town.

Sacramento tried to fill the void with tough forward Ron Artest (later known as Metta World Peace), the 2004 NBA Defensive Player of the Year. It was not enough to prevent Sacramento from posting mediocre records the next three seasons. In 2006-07, the Kings missed the playoffs entirely for the first time in nine years.

After another losing campaign in 2007–08, Sacramento set about rebuilding, adding such players as rookie forward Jason Thompson, who impressed teammates with his hustle and touch around the basket. "I saw quite a bit of his tape, and I had talked to the coaching

staff," said Artest. "I knew he was going to be a good player."

Artest would not be around long enough to see if his predictions came true, though. The Kings traded him for veteran point guard Bobby Jackson and forward Donte Green. Although young guard Kevin Martin poured in points in bunches, and veteran center Brad Miller worked the boards hard, the Kings endured a 17–65 season in 2008–09. Fortunately, Sacramento struck gold in the 2009 NBA Draft. New shooting guard Tyreke Evans promptly led the club with 20.1 points per game and earned the

INTRODUCING...

CHRIS WEBBER

POSITION FORWARD
HEIGHT 6-FOOT-9
KINGS SEASONS
1998-2005

Chris Webber had made a name for himself as a member of the "Fab Five" (a group of five outstanding freshmen in the 1991–92 season) at the University of Michigan and as a solid player with the Golden State Warriors and Washington Bullets before being traded to the Kings. Initially, Webber was not interested in reporting to Sacramento because he didn't want to go to such a small city and a team with Sacramento's losing history. He warmed to the place, though, as the franchise added such players as center Vlade Divac. The union benefited both sides. The Kings improved dramatically, and Webber's career took off. The brawny forward earned All-Star status 5 times and averaged a career-best 27.1 points in 2000–01. Webber was also a top-tier rebounder, and Kings head coach Rick Adelman made sure the team took advantage of his slick passing skills by running much of the offense through him. "It was a great and special time," Webber later said of his Sacramento seasons. "We didn't get that title, but it was still an awesome team."

TYREKE EVANS USED SPEED AND SMOOTH MOVES TO WEAVE TO THE HOOP THROUGH TRAFFIC.

43

CLOSE BUT NO CIGAR

The Kings' 2001–02 season was one of the greatest in franchise history. At the start of the year, Sacramento switched point guards by trading Jason Williams to the Vancouver Grizzlies for Mike Bibby, a move that helped spark the team to a franchise-best 61–21 record and had the Kings and their fans dreaming about an NBA championship. After Bibby, star forward Chris Webber, and the rest of the Kings won two playoff series, they met the Los Angeles Lakers in the Western Conference finals, a bruising, back-and-forth series that came down to a deciding Game 7 played in Sacramento. In the fourth quarter, Bibby nailed two free throws to tie the game 100–100 and send it into overtime. The extra session belonged to the Lakers, though, as center Shaquille O'Neal and his teammates ran away to a 112–106 win. With the bitter defeat, the Kings became the first NBA team in 20 years to lose a Game 7 playoff contest at home. "It hurts. It really hurts big," Bibby said. "We should have closed it out when we had the opportunity."

2010 NBA Rookie of the Year award—the first time in more than 30 years that a member of the franchise had received that honor. Sacramento improved to 25–57, not good enough to reach the playoffs. But new coach Paul Westphal liked the team's young core of Evans, Thompson, and guard Beno Udrih. "The journey is just beginning," Westphal said.

nfortunately, the trail was rough in 2010–11, as the Kings went just 24–58 despite adding their top draft choice, DeMarcus Cousins. The 6-foot-11 center from the University of Kentucky averaged 14.1 points and 8.6 rebounds while being named to the NBA All-Rookie First Team. During the 2011 NBA Draft, the Kings traded for the rights to National College Player of the Year Jimmer Fredette, a prolific scorer who made an immediate impact on the team's bottom line. "Jimmermania" generated a 540 percent increase in sales of team clothing and other merchandise. Diminutive guard Isaiah Thomas (standing just 5-foot-9) delivered the goods in 2011–12, starting 37 games while averaging 11.5 points and 4.1 assists. Two-time NBA Rookie of the Month Thomas was convinced he was where he was supposed to be. "People still say I can't play at this level and I won't be in the league that long," Thomas said. "All of that motivates me." Despite Thomas's achievements and further improvement from Cousins, Sacramento finished with a 22–44 mark.

Persistent relocation rumors turned serious midway through the 2012–13 season when a group of well-heeled Seattle businessmen planned to purchase the team. However, investors led by Sacramento billionaire Vivek Ranadive made a counteroffer to keep the Kings in Sacramento and to do whatever was necessary to return the team to contention. After the Kings finished 28–54, hiring longtime assistant coach Mike Malone as head coach represented the first step in that direction. "Malone inherits a talented young roster in Sacramento headlined by volatile center DeMarcus Cousins that has yet to blend—or play defense," noted AP sportswriter Antonio Gonzalez.

More changes followed. Before the 2013–14 season, the Kings traded Evans and added new faces such as guard Ben McLemore, the seventh overall NBA Draft pick. But hopes of a winning campaign soon ebbed away, and the roster shuffling continued with midseason trades that brought in top-tier forwards Derrick Williams and Rudy Gay to combine with the offensive punch of Cousins and Thomas. The two stars seemed to be just the boost the franchise needed for the road ahead.

Under original owner/coach Les Harrison, the Royals were perennial playoff contenders and took the NBA title in 1951. But the franchise has the dubious distinction of having gone the longest without a championship of any NBA team. A number of NBA experts believed that Ranadive was capable of stemming the recent tide of mediocrity, thanks to his success in improving the Golden State Warriors as a minority owner. "When you think about the team's turnaround the last couple of years, it's one of the most impressive ones in sports," said Sacramento mayor Kevin Johnson. Sacramento fans hope that their team's new owner can do the same thing in the state capital and end the long trophy drought.

DeMARCUS COUSINS POSTED BIG STATISTICS, BUT HIS ATTITUDE PROBLEMS DIVIDED FANS.

INDEX